MW00572409

PASSION
FOR
ISRAEL

Other Books by Daniel C. Juster, Th.D.

Dynamics of Spiritual Deception

Due Process – A Plea for Biblical Justice Among God's People

Growing to Maturity – A Messianic Jewish Guide

Israel, the Church, and the Last Days

Jewish Roots – A Foundation of Biblical Theology

Jewishness and Jesus

Passover: The Key that Unlocks the Book of Revelation

Relational Leadership – A Manual of Leadership Principles for
Congregational Leaders and Members

That They May Be One – A Brief Review of Church Restoration
Movements and Their Connection to the Jewish People

The Irrevocable Calling – Israel's Role As A Light to the Nations

PASSION
FOR
ISRAEL

A Short History of the
Evangelical Church's
Commitment to the
Jewish People and Israel

Daniel C. Juster, Th.D.

Lederer Books
A division of
Messianic Jewish Publishers
Clarksville, MD 21029

15 14 13 12   5 4 3 2 1

Library of Congress Control Number: 2012935986

ISBN 978-1-936716-40-1

Printed in the United States of America
Copyright © 2012 by Daniel C. Juster, Th.D.

Published by
Lederer Books
A division of
Messianic Jewish Publishers
6120 Day Long Lane
Clarksville, Maryland 21029

Distributed by
Messianic Jewish Resources Int'l.
www.messianicjewish.net
Individual and Trade Order line: (800) 410-7367
Email: lederer@messianicjewish.net

CONTENTS

INTRODUCTION

This book is written to address two misconceptions that are widespread and very destructive. One is that commitment to the Jews as God's chosen people is the creation of John Nelson Darby and his Dispensational Theology from the mid 19th century. It is then argued that this is an aberration. This assertion is a gross distortion of history. The special commitment of Christians to the Jews as God's still elect people has a long history stretching back to the Reformation. This important history is a story that needs to be told to shore up the stand of those Christians who are committed to the Jewish people and to gain new adherents to the cause.

1

The second distortion is that Jewish community leaders sometimes argue that Christian love for the Jews has been proven to be fickle. It is asserted that Christians have always turned against the Jews after evangelistic efforts failed. This is a gross distortion of history as well, for there is a long and important Protestant story where this has never been the case. A minor key that comes from this false argument is that for any Christian support for the Jews to be seen as authentic love, Christians must repudiate efforts to see Jews come to faith in Yeshua. In addition, they must reject the Messianic Jews, Jews who believe in Jesus and still live and identify as Jews. This is an unfair stand. This book will seek to address this issue in its last pages.

We truly live in amazing times. While ethnic and religious conflicts persist into the 21st century, one of the most remarkable movements in our times is a Christian world reconciliation movement. Most of the people involved in these efforts have become networked together. There have been reconciliation walks with repentance for sins against Muslims and Jews during the Crusades. American efforts have sought reconciliation between white and black Christians and between those of European descent and Native Americans. Australian efforts toward the Aborigines have taken place as well as New Zealand efforts toward the Maoris. The ministry of Jesus the Messiah as being one of reconciliation between God and man, and man and man, is being taken seriously.

Many seek to first bring the Christians together, who belong to these divided groups, to apply the blood of the Lamb in repentance. However, such efforts have gone beyond this to include many who are not professing Christians. John Dawson, who leads the International Reconciliation Coalition, has given himself fully to such efforts. His book, *Healing America's Wounds*, provides both a theological rationale and case histories of effects. He is presently writing many booklets for reconciliation among the ethnic and religious groups where the conflicts are greatest.

In John Dawson's book there is an important statement that the greatest wound in history is the wound between Israel (the Jewish people) and the Church. He claims that healing this wound will bring the greatest spiritual benefit to the world. It is my conviction that healing this wound will require greater listening and understanding. If Christians and Jews misrepresent each other, we will not see great progress.

In humility we can make progress. Three events marked the desire to publish this book. First was the publication in the *Washington Jewish Week* of what was called the most important events of the last 1000 years in Jewish history. This list included both Jewish achievements and terrible atrocities at the hands of those who called themselves Christians. No events of a positive character between Christians toward Jews were noted. Yet there have been many such events which have been world changing. Why would these be left out? Is the wound too great to admit any good?

Second, was the reaction of the American Jewish Community to Southern Baptist efforts to evangelize specific groups by creating literature geared to each group (Jews, Moslems and Hindus) for a great Chicago outreach. To the Jewish people, these efforts are seen as near to persecution. Targeting Jews is said to be wrong. To the Baptists, such efforts merely seek to communicate the gospel more effectively through understanding the Jewish, Muslim and Hindu communities; all who ask different questions and have different concerns which the Gospel needs to address specifically. As the late Black evangelist Tom Skinner was fond of saying, "Many say, 'Jesus is the answer,' but I want to know, 'What is the question?'"

Evangelism needs to answer the questions that arise from those to whom the message is spoken. The word "target" is loaded; we should rather use the word *specific evangelism*. A too generalized message appeals to few. This is the common understanding of all missions. The culmination of this debate came on the Larry King show where two Jewish leaders debated with David Brickner, the Director of Jews for Jesus, and with the head of a Southern Baptist Theological Seminary. What a debate it was! Both spoke out of their own commitments. However, one statement by one of the Jewish leaders was very noteworthy.

After the Baptist leader professed that Baptists love the Jewish people, the Jewish leaders said it was the wrong kind of love, contingent upon Jews coming to faith in Jesus. When such does not occur, as usual in history, the Christians turn against the Jews. Is this true? Has this been the nature of the history? In America? Where Christians professed to love the Jewish people? Is there documentation? It certainly happened in Catholic Europe that Jews who did not convert were persecuted, from the early Middle Ages to recent days before the Catholic and State marriage ended! It happened in Luther's day, with a former positive Luther (in *Jesus was a Jew*) turning against the

Jewish people in his later life (*The Jews and their Lies*). Yet has it been true of most of Protestant Christian history? Is such anti-Semitism the whole story?

In addition there is the question of replacement theology or supercessionism. Basically, this theology teaches that the Jewish nation as God's covenant people has been fully replaced by the Church and is no longer the chosen people of God. Either the Jews are seen as like all other nations or they are seen as lesser because they had their chance to receive the Gospel and rejected it. This was the classical view in the theology of Roman Catholicism, Eastern Orthodoxy, classical Lutheran theology formulated in the 18th century, and in Reformed thought of the 18th and 19th century. This does not mean that no one from these traditions had regard for the Jewish people, who were the chosen people, and concern for their welfare and civil rights. It does not mean that all in these streams agreed with this viewpoint of replacement. This would be to paint with too broad a brush. However, an amazing development in the 19th and 20 century is the official repudiation of replacement theology. The most noteworthy is the new Roman Catholic position in *Nostre Atetae* in Vatican Council II. This document is now reflected in the *New Catholic Catechism (1995)*, which clearly and forcefully affirms the chosenness of the Jewish people, the continued validity of Jewish life and much more. Other Protestant groups have followed with parallel repudiations.

However, there is another story that has rarely been told. This is a story of an historic Christian movement that has become dominant in American Protestant Christianity. It is a movement I call Evangelical Pietism.

In Evangelical Pietism, I find the roots of affirming the continued chosenness of the Jewish people and a repudiation of replacement theology. Evangelical Pietism had a strong commitment to the view that salvation is based on faith in the crucified and risen Messiah, Jesus. All men and women, including the Jewish people needed to heed the call of the Gospel for salvation. Out of love for men and women and their conviction that peoples were lost without Jesus, Evangelical Pietist missionaries bled and died to bring the Good News to the far corners of the world. However, because no one could know the time of one's response, Evangelical Pietists did not turn on those who rejected or did not yet receive the message.

Not only was this true for many peoples, but also especially true of the Jewish people because most Evangelical Pietists believed that the Jews were a chosen people. Love and respect were due to them. Contrary to what the Jewish leaders said to Larry King, *I know of no incident of Evangelical Pietists turning against the Jews (for over 400 years) when they did not accept the message.* The Evangelical Pietist movements have a good record toward the Jewish people for the most part. So do the peace churches, the Anabaptists (Mennonites, Brethren groups, etc.).

Evangelical Pietists could never see the call of all to be saved in Jesus as either hateful or narrow. For them the evidence of the truth of the Gospel was so very clear. Once again, contrary to the misperceptions, those who preached heaven and hell were not hateful toward those who did not receive the message. Jew and Gentile were called. However, because all were seen as terribly distant from God, fallen far short of his standard, only the received righteousness though the Messiah Jesus could justify Jew and Gentile before God. This is a message that arises from the New Testament. There were some who espoused a wider hope, like John Wesley. He believed that some could be connected to the Messiah Jesus unawares in a prevenient grace way if they responded to the "light that lights every man." (John 1:9). Yet, because most do not so respond to natural revelation, Methodists were not lacking in zeal to spread the Gospel.

Here then is an amazing truth, that these who were very black and white concerning the claims of the Gospel upon all were also the most loving of Christians toward the Jewish people. I am not claiming by this that there were no Christians in Evangelical Pietist groups who were not anti-Semitic in attitude; nor that no anti-Semitism was shown to Jewish people by some. What I am claiming is that the overwhelming thrust of Evangelical Pietism has been pro-Jewish. This does not mean that when they come together in repentance that those from such backgrounds do not repent. They own the history before the Evangelical Pietists as their own and repent for all attitudes and deeds in their midst that have been contrary to the One who gave himself for us. However, it is to say to the Jewish people that Evangelical Pietism is not the place for your fears to be grounded. This is very little understood in the Jewish community, which often does not make distinctions among various varieties of Christianity.

What is Evangelical Pietism? Evangelical Pietism is rooted in seventeenth century Puritanism. It spread and influenced the Lutheran Pietists in Germany and then into Scandinavia. This in turn was the influence on the amazing Moravian movement under Count Ludwig Nicholas Von Zinzendorf. The Moravians were a great influence upon the Methodists and upon some Anglicans. Free Churches from Scandinavia derived their roots from Pietism (Evangelical Free Church, Evangelical Covenant Church, Swedish Baptist Church, etc.). Baptists derived from the Puritans but were later influenced by Pietists as well. From this came revivalism and a host of American denominations such as the holiness denominations (Nazarenes and Christian Missionary Alliance) and Pentecostal denominations. It is my contention that such groups, which now dominate American Protestantism, have historically been pro-Jewish. For them it is a doctrinal issue. I am using the term Evangelical Pietism in a new sense, that is those movements that have roots in the historically understood movements called Pietism, even if they today would not designate themselves as Evangelical Pietists, but as Baptists, Pentecostals, Free Church adherents, New Apostolic Movements, Nazarenes, Christian Missionary Alliance Churches, Independent Bible Churches and others.

I would be remiss if I did not mention one other factor. Many groups among Evangelical Pietists have known persecutions in the "old country." They have seen the danger of state power used to back or establish a particular state church. Therefore, they have stood against the state church and have called for a separation of civil government and church government. Rabbi Eliezer Berkowitz in his monumental study, *Faith After the Holocaust*, argues that the problem has not been Christianity as much as the State seeking to establish order through a state religion. In his view, religious persecution is very limited where there is not such a conjoining of power. Others have also seen that Evangelical Pietists are friends of the Jewish people and that their influence on society is good for the Jewish people (e.g. Dennis Prager and Rabbi Daniel Lapin). These are a minority, for most do not penetrate Christianity to even distinguish Evangelical Pietism.

So with these introductory comments in mind, I now seek to develop the theme of this book. Three sources are especially important in this study. The first is *The Puritan Hope* by Ian Murray. In this wonderful study, Murray shows the nature of Puritan eschatology (doctrine of the last days). For most Puritan exegetes, Israel was preserved to be re-ingrafted into their own olive tree (Romans 11:16-24)). Their preservation shows a chosenness that has not been exhausted. A minority was even Zionist, holding to a return of the Jewish people to the land of Israel. He shows the Puritans to be more revivalist and less stodgy than usually perceived.

The second is *Israel's Friend* by Oscar Skarsaunae. Dr. Skarsaunae was dean of the Lutheran Theological Seminary in Oslo, Norway when he first gave me a copy of his book. Sadly, this book is only in Norwegian. His book documents the nature of the Lutheran Pietists in Germany and the influence of these Pietists and Moravians on Scandinavia. This influence continues to this day. The last is an amazing book by a traditional Jewish leader, Franz Kobler, entitled *The Vision Was There*.

Evangelical Pietism, as we will note in further detail has great variety and some features we might see as good and others as not so good. However there is a broad set of beliefs and values in Evangelical Pietism that produces people who are pro-Jewish at best and tolerant at worst. Few are anti-Semitic. It is my contention that where Evangelical Pietism is strong the Jewish people find friends and allies for their rights in society.

CHAPTER ONE

PURITAN ROOTS

The Puritan movement was a movement primarily in England and the American Colonies, which sought to purify the Church. Puritans were concerned with what they perceived to be compromises in Anglicanism: unqualified clergy, a wrong conformity, and a still too Roman Catholic orientation in doctrine and practice. Puritans were of many varieties. Some were committed to stay within the Church of England and accepted the government of Bishops. Others were desirous of reforming the Church to Presbyterian government and doctrine. For a time they prevailed in England. Others wanted a Congregationalist form of government. They prevailed in New England. The

Pilgrims were a particular sub-group of Puritans known as separatists. We know them as the ones who came to Plymouth, Massachusetts in 1620 on the Mayflower. Other Puritans were not separatists. In England, the Puritans prevailed. King Charles I and Archbishop Laud were executed after an awful civil war. Lord Oliver Cromwell and his New Model Army prevailed. He became the Lord Protector of England. During this time of Puritan rule, the *Westminster Confession* was composed to provide unity of doctrine and practice for the churches. In general Puritans were interested in conformity in society, just not that of the Anglican stripe. Oliver Cromwell was more tolerant. When the monarchy and the Archbishop were reestablished after the death of Cromwell, Puritan thought continued as an influence in the Church of England.

Puritans in America and England were Calvinists. They had strong views on predestination, on the nature of society, the Law of God and the vocation of all believers. As noted, the Puritans were conformists. While they would tolerate others of a different belief if they kept quiet about it, all were required to tithe to the Church, and the officers of the State enforced Church discipline. One of the great stories is how freedom of religion evolved from Puritan conformity in much of New England and Great Britain. On the British side of the ocean, people were simply worn out by religious controversy. King Charles II ordered toleration for religious minorities and an end to persecution. This did not mean that England was ready to embrace a Roman Catholic leaning King. This was one of the reasons for the removal of James II who succeeded Charles II. England would be tolerant, but would not allow any but a Protestant majority and an Anglican King to rule. Hence James II was deposed and William and Mary came from Holland in the Glorious Revolution. Now England would be officially Anglican, but tolerant of other sects and Scotland would be Presbyterian, but tolerant. Ireland would pose another problem, which we see until this day. We should note that other Calvinists on the Continent did not necessarily embrace Puritan emphases.

Puritans were committed to Bible study with accurate exegesis at a level not previously seen in the Church. They believed that progressive revivals would lead to the return of Jesus. Because they took the Bible straightforwardly, they could not gainsay the promises of God to Israel, the Jewish people.

The Puritans in general believed in the preservation of the Jewish people and a bright and glorious end to their long journey. This great end would come at the end of time, but required kindness in the present order. Yes, that destiny was seen to culminate when Israel embraced the Messiah Jesus as her own. Some even believed in the regathering of the Jewish people to the Land.

Thomas Brightman was one of the first to write more fully on the themes of Jewish restoration. He lived from 1562-1607. Franz Kobler calls him the father of the British doctrine of the restoration of the Jews. In his book *A Revelation of the Revelation*, he argued that the Anti-Christ (identified with Rome) would be overthrown. Then would be seen the calling of the Jewish people who would return to Palestine, restoring their Kingdom. They would embrace Jesus as the Messiah and their kingdom would be restored. "Shall they return to Jerusalem again?" Brightman asks, "There is nothing more certain: the prophets do everywhere confirm it and beat upon it." He also predicted that the whole east would be in obedience and subjection unto the Jews. Theologian Giles Fletcher followed Brightman in this. Thomas Draxe was another contemporary of Brightman who wrote

The World's Resurrection or the Calling of the Jews—A familiar Commentary upon the eleventh Chapter of Saint Paul to the Romans (1608). He considered the preservation of the scattered Jewish people as an amazing miracle, which would lead to their regathering and coming to Jesus as the Messiah. Sir Henry Finch, a noted layman and Sergeant-at-law echoed these themes. He had great repute in jurisprudence, a Member of Parliament for many years and wrote *The World's Great Restoration.* His great vision was of a restored Jewish commonwealth. "They shall live in safety and continue to stay there for ever." Some Puritans would believe in a future for Israel in the New Heavens and New Earth, but most would not accept the views of literal millennium as in Finch. Archbishop William Laud greatly criticized Finch and his views. The famous logician and philosopher Francis Bacon was influenced greatly by Finch's views.

It should be noted that these writers were taking a new and more accurate view of Romans 11. Romans 9-11 gives Paul's great explanation of the future of Israel and the answer to the great question that if Jesus is the Messiah, why does not Israel believe it? He argues both that it is a result of God's providence and of Jewish error. However, it is temporary. The hardening has happened

17

in part until the full number of Gentiles will come in. So all Israel would be saved. "Though they are enemies of the Gospel, they are beloved and elect for the sake of the Fathers, for the gifts and call of God (to Israel) are irrevocable." (Rom. 11:26-29) Indeed, Israel's full acceptance would be life from the dead. (Rom. 11:15) This view of Romans 11 was a foundation of Puritan thought according to Murray. Some of these were Anglicans who were setting a foundation for Puritan exegesis. Previously many Church theologians had argued that Israel in Romans 11 sometimes referred to spiritual Israel and that "All Israel would be saved" meant that all true Christians would be saved. Those elect were either Gentile Christians or those Jews who believed and became Christians. To the Puritans this exegesis was ludicrous, an attempt to avoid the plain meaning of the text.

We find as a result that 17th century Puritans were passionate and persistent in their defense of the continued chosenness of the Jewish people, God's will in their preservation and in their ultimate re-ingrafting to one olive tree. Samuel Rutherford, the famous author of the book *Lex Rex,* Law is King, wrote passionately concerning their meeting with Jesus at his return. How the tears would flow as they finally embrace as brothers and receive Him as King! Rutherford's writing urges love and kindness toward this ancient people, for if God loves them, how shall we do other? Rutherford was greatly noted in his day for his political writing and argument that all are to be subject to the Law from God as the basis to overcome tyranny. Elnathan Parr also so wrote in a brilliant commentary on Romans. In it he takes to task all replacement theologians and shows why Israel and the Jews in Romans 9-11 is none other than the same subject, the Jewish people. His arguments are so well put forth that we are amazed that any would hold to another point of view. So also were the views of Increase Mather in Massachusetts in his *Commentary on Romans 9-11*. Here are the same arguments as Parr. Jonathan Edwards, a century later, would also write in the same way as Parr and Mather. He is usually considered the greatest thinker in American history, the defender of the First Great Awakening and a careful exegete. Other writers are too numerous to describe. We can name John Archer in *The Personal Reign of Christ Upon Earth*, 1642 (a literal millennium view); Robert Merton in *Israel's Redemption,* and writers Nathaniel Holmes, James Durham and Henry Jessey, *The Glory of Judah and Israel* (a Baptist and founder of the earliest Welsh Church). The last was the first to collect funds for needy Jews in Palestine. Sir Oliver Cromwell himself believed that God would bring His people again from the depths of the sea.

We should especially note the writings of Johann Amos Comenius (Komensky), the Bishop of the Bohemian Brethren. The Bohemian Brethren, in the areas now known as the Czech Republic, Slovakia, and parts of Hungary, stem from the early Reformation of John Hus. They were accepted as true in doctrine and practice by both Lutherans and Reformed movements in Northern Europe. Later Count Ludwig Von Zinzendorf would reconstitute this Church and claim to be in line with its bishops in apostolic descent. This movement was mostly destroyed by the persecuting Catholic State. Today it has been reconstituted in these lands. In 1642 Comenius, having been invited to England to effect reforms in Education (he was a great educator), wrote *The Way of Light*. This book argues for universal education as well as the restoration of the Jews preceding the coming of the Messiah. All nations would embrace a single faith, and would turn towards the light of a divinely restored Zion.

The great narrative poet himself, John Milton, also argued for the restoration of the Jews, as reflected in

Paradise Regained. Milton was a friend of religious liberty and a good friend of Roger Williams who founded Rhode Island, the first colony to practice liberty. In his great work he quotes Jesus in the temptation responding to Satan,

> Yet at length, time to himself best known,
> Remembering Abraham, by some wondrous call
> May bring them back repentant and sincere,
> And at their passing cleave the Assyrian Flood,
> While to their native land with joy they haste,
> As the Red Sea and Jordan once He cleft,
> When to the Promised Land their fathers pass'd
> To his due time and providence I leave them.

Milton had no doubts of this event according to Franz Kobler. Many passages in his theological work *De Doctrina Christiana* repeat the same themes.

These Puritan ideas led to a desire to see the Jewish people invited back to Great Britain. They had been expelled in the 13th century during the days of Richard the Lionhearted. Cromwell himself desired this restoration but did not live to see it, though it happened shortly after he died. American Puritans also desired to invite the Jewish people to live in the

Colonies. The American Puritans saw their history as similar to Jewish history. Their passage over the ocean was parallel to the passage through the Red Sea. They saw themselves as a New Israel, but not replacing the Old. Though they would not yet give religious freedom to all, the Jewish people, who honored the Law of God, were seen as an exception. Some other writings are also noteworthy. Samuel Lee wrote *Israel Redux or the Restoration of Israel,* which discusses the juridical, historical and geographic premises of a return. This orientation spilled over to the continent where French Protestant Pierre Jurieu wrote on similar themes in his *L'Accomplissement des Propheties.* He expected the return at the end of the 17th century. Dutch visionary Holger Paulli sought to influence King William II to conquer Palestine and to become the Cyrus of the Jewish people. So Thomas Barnett presented the restoration of the Jewish people as the climax of an inevitable world process. He rejected political means to accomplish this, but greatly aided in establishing this hope.

In 1648, Baptists Johanna Cartwright, and her son Ebenezer and Edward Nicholas, in his *Apology for the Honourable Nation of the Jews, and all the Sons of Israel,* called upon their fellow citizens to show themselves "compassionate and helpers of the afflicted Jews." Many Jews needed a refuge as Marranos were fleeing Spain and Portugal, and Jewish people in droves were fleeing from the Cossacks in Ukraine, who were led by the butcher Chmielnitzky. At this time, the view became established that the restoration of the Jewish people to England could be preparation for their return to the land of Israel. John Dury argued for this readmission in *A Case of Conscience, whether it be lawful to admit Jews into a Christian Commonwealth?* In 1655 despite Cromwell's eloquent plea, the admission was denied. *Marranos* who had settled in England later confessed their faith openly and petitioned the government for religious freedom. It was granted. Charles II within a decade readmitted the Jewish people to England. The Colonies would also be open to the Jewish people who would find great favor in North America. One must recognize that these Puritan roots prepared for the settlement of the Jews in the United States and led to the most prosperous and free Jewish community since the Commonwealth of Israel.

Some Puritans saw the terrible results of state religious persecution. They espoused a radical idea of freedom and were also very favorable to the civil rights of Jews settling in their midst. One of the earliest of these was Roger Williams. He had become a Baptist, and even had some contact with Anabaptists in the European Continent. He was banished from Massachusetts and Connecticut for his non-conformity, but later was given a charter for the colony of Rhode Island. Williams was a perfectionist and though he founded the first Baptist Church in the colonies, he could not find peace in the imperfections of Church life. His more enduring contribution was in politics and the importance of religious freedom. He envisioned a state under a common law that various Christian sects could accept, including the Jewish people. Williams envisioned a state where Jew and Christian could live together in peace. He was deeply religious and hated persecution as destroying true faith. Though becoming a Baptist and Arminian (Free will was seen as a greater factor in salvation and not predestination.) his own Puritan roots were certainly an influence on this great 17th century leader.

We now leave the Puritan period, but note that their influence continued. John Locke, the great philosopher who influenced the founding fathers of the United States wrote a Commentary on Paul's Epistles and said, "God is able to collect them into one Body . . . and set them in flourishing condition in their own land." Famous scientist Isaac Newton also wrote passionately on these themes. William Whitston who translated Josephus also looked for the Millennium and the restoration of the Jews. These Puritan influences had great effect in Evangelical Anglican circles. Bishop Joseph Butler in his *Analogy of Religion* (1732), the standard textbook of Apologetics in Britain for 150 years, made much of the scattering and preservation of the Jewish people as a proof of Biblical authority and accuracy. He then predicted, on the basis of Scripture, the full restoration of the Jewish people to their land and to faith in Jesus the Messiah. However, it is now time to leave the Puritans and England and America and go to the continent.

CHAPTER TWO

EVANGELICAL PIETISM IN EUROPE

A great movement began in Europe that has followers to this day. It is called Lutheran Pietism. The founder of this movement was Jacob Philip Spenner. His colleague August Hermann Franke was also a foundational figure and made the University of Halle a center for Lutheran Pietism. Many evaluations of Pietism have been given. For some Pietism is associated with legalistic rectitude. For others it is known for its iconoclasticism, for the radical Pietists eschewed stained glass and ritual as corruptions of simple faith. These excesses were unfortunate and are not to be found in the early fathers of the movement nor is it characteristic of the broad stream. Some in Scandinavia still see themselves as Lutheran Pietists and other Lutherans reject the label.

The Pietists read the literature of the Puritans, especially the devotional literature. However, they reapplied this literature in a Lutheran context, less predestinarian and less systematic than the Puritans. Out of their seeking and devotion, the Pietists developed what Oskar Skarsaunae describes as four foundations. The first was a deep devotional life that was to be the characteristic of every believer. This devotional life was to center on Jesus as the crucified and risen Messiah. It was to be both the individual and the corporate emphasis. It was religion of the heart, not only of the mind in its logic and doctrine. As Jonathan Edwards would argue in his masterpiece *The Religious Affections*, Christianity was in essence an affectionate relationship between God and Man, the Messiah Jesus and his people. This was to include mind and emotions, the motions of the heart. With the emphasis of Edwards, the Pietists would certainly agree. This emphasis centered lovingly on the Messiah's suffering for us.

The second emphasis was the Unity of the Church. The Pietists wanted to see unity among all who truly loved the Messiah Jesus. They saw the emphasis of John 17:21 as eschatological, namely that the Church would be one before the second coming of Jesus. "That they may be one as We are one, that the world may believe that You have sent me." The Pietists looked for an evangelical unity between Lutheran and Reformed (they were fed by Puritans), and Anglicans. Pietists met in homes to encourage one another to devotional life and witness.

The third emphasis was world missions. Pietists longed to see the Gospel spread to people who had not yet received it. Even today Pietist prayer bands to support world missions exist in Scandinavian countries, for Pietism spread from Germany to Norway, Sweden, Denmark and Finland. The flame would become so dim in Germany as to be almost extinguished in the 20th Century, but it still burned in Scandinavia in the 20th century and to this day.

The fourth emphasis is usually left out when people talk about Pietism, but it was foundational. It was a commitment and love for the Jewish people and prayer and witness toward their salvation. Some among the Pietists would become supporters of the return of the Jewish people to the land of Israel. They would become explicitly involved in real efforts in the 19th century. However at this point, we are still writing about the early 18th century.

One of the great Lutheran Pietists was Count Ludwig Von Zinzendorf. He adopted the same four stands, but spread them with even greater influence and practical involvement in the 18th century. Zinzendorf founded a community for the purpose of living out these four emphases. It was called Hernhutt. All true believers who lived by these emphases were welcome, whether Lutheran, Reformed or even Catholic. In the first chapter we spoke of Comenius, the bishop of the United Brethren, *Unitus Fratrum,* from Bohemia. These were the spiritual descendants of John Hus. Zinzendorf found himself receiving a persecuted remnant of these brethren into Hernhutt. As his ranks filled with these folks, a challenge was posed to him. Would he become involved in saving this ancient Protestant Church that preceded Luther and Calvin. Yes, and eventually Zinzendorf himself was consecrated a Bishop in this fellowship though a succession that went back to Comenius. Zinzendorf reconstituted the Brethren as the Moravian Church. He so desired unity that he sought to make his Church the servant of other churches. If there were a church in an area that would live out the truths of the Moravians, then he would not plant one. He would send out groups to serve the churches in the purposes of unity and missions. To the Anglicans he could claim a real apostolic succession. To the Lutherans, he emphasized justification by faith. To the Reformed, he demonstrated that the Bishop was not monarchical but subject to elders who governed the Church. Truly this was unique in Church history. Yet what was also noteworthy was the passionate love for the Jewish people shared by Moravian and Pietist. Cold formality was rejected in all spiritual realms, and no less so in this concern.

The Moravians were amazing prayer warriors and gave themselves to a chain of continuous prayer for 100 years. They sent missionaries all over the world. Many gave up their lives; but others followed with dauntless courage. The Moravians influenced many other streams. They came to Pennsylvania in the person of Zinzendorf himself and sought to unite the different sects to cooperative and practical unity. They came into England and influenced early Methodism. It was John Wesley's contact with the Moravians on board his cross Atlantic trip that led him to that experiential Christianity that warmed his heart.

Though the Methodists did not remain within the Moravian stream, for they had their own vision and method, they were greatly influenced nevertheless and cooperation between Methodists and Moravians was common.

So great was the influence of Pietism in Scandinavia that all four emphases swept the churches. The emphasis on loving the Jewish people and praying for their salvation was pronounced. This included a hope for their return to the land of Israel. The emphases of the Pietists and Moravians would influence many other denominations that could trace their roots to them. We indeed see such influences stemming from the Puritans on most Baptist groups as well.

Methodism was really a Pietist movement in England and among Anglicans. They followed similar small group models. The Wesleys had the same hope for the salvation of the Jewish people and knew their preservation was promised by God. Though the Methodists were forced out of the Anglican Church after John Wesley's death, Methodist influences had continued effect upon many. We find this hope enshrined in the hymns of Charles Wesley. Both the Millennium and the restoration of the Jewish people to their land are expressed. The Wesleyan hymnal is Methodist theology sung. The Evangelist Phillip Doddridge also wrote of this restoration. Again, we can see the influence on the Anglicans for Bishop Richard Hurd wrote in a similar way. During this same period, Samuel Collet wrote *Treatise on the Future Restoration of the Jews and Israelites to their own Land* (1746). He looked for agricultural settlements and that a few would to lead to further growth in the population and more would then return. This was quite prophetic. It should not be thought that these trends were unopposed, but the momentum continued to gain on into the 19th century.

Debate ensued as to whether or not restoration would take place before Jewish conversion to Jesus or after. There were proponents on both sides, but the idea of restoration to the Land coming first prevailed. John Gill, John Jortin, and Robert Lowth (Bishop of London) argued that the conversion would come first. Joseph Eyre and the famous naturalist and philosopher Joseph Priestly argued that the restoration to the Land would come first. The problem here is that Scripture lends itself to both interpretations and can be read in different ways. Priestly wrote a plea that the Jews would acknowledge Jesus as the Messiah but also added the prayer that, "The God of Heaven, the God of Abraham, Isaac and Jacob whom we Christians as well as you worship (and whom we have learned from you to worship) may be graciously pleased to put an end to your sufferings, gather you from all nations, resettle you in your own country, the land of Canaan, and make you the most illustrious . . .of all the nations on earth."

These emphases would culminate in practical Christian Zionism, which would have an overwhelming importance for Jewish history and world history.

CHAPTER THREE

THE NINETEENTH CENTURY CULMINATION

The nineteenth century and early 20th century would see the triumph of the idea of the restoration of Israel, the birth of many new pietist denominations (denominations that have their roots in pietism, Methodism, and the earlier Puritan ideas that influenced the Lutheran Pietists), and the political actions, which would lead to the eventual birth of the Jewish state. Though such Christian Zionists desired to see Jewish people believe in Jesus, their commitment to the Jewish people was not contingent on Jewish conversion. Indeed, they understood that the majority of Israel would not believe in Jesus until the end of this Age. Their love for and commitment to the Jewish people was a clear doctrinal matter, which would not change according to the vicissitudes of history.

The 18th century closed with Napoleon invading Palestine and issuing a proclamation for the Jewish people to return to their land. This stirred those who had this hope of return fixed in their theology. Many took up the pen, including Joseph Priestly again, praying for the dissolution of the Turkish Empire so the Jewish people might return to what he called a land "Silent, without inhabitants, it is wholly uncultivated, empty and ready to receive you." It was not to be at this time. Yet Napoleon's ventures seemed to bring this hope to near fulfillment. In many, this restoration was connected to their conversion to believe in Jesus, either before, after or simultaneously.

George Stanley Faber (1773-1854) became the outstanding apologist of the restoration idea. Many others continued writing on this theme. Faber held that France would fail in restoring the Jewish people, but England would succeed, and that their conversion would be part of this restoration. Other writers such as Edward Irving, William Cunningham, and Hugh McNeile added to the literature. One writer stated in anonymous complaint,

"That the doctrine of Israel's restoration to Palestine is a popular one—that it has been favored by some of the wisest, most learned, and best men in the Church of Christ, and that it is still maintained by the majority of Christians." In 1807, the London Society for Promoting Christianity among the Jews was established. One of their tenets was that the "restoration of the Jews . . .will be faithfully accomplished."

Lewis Way, another committed worker for restoration was able to present this hope at the Aix-la-Chapelle conference in 1818 to discuss a European settlement after Napoleon's fall. The Russian Tsar also wanted this to be discussed. The sentiments were even found in the poetry of William Blake:

> England awake! Awake! Awake!
> Jerusalem thy sister calls!
> Why will those sleep the sleep of death
>   And close her from thy ancient walls?

Lord Byron also wrote a series of poems also supporting restoration in his *Hebrew Melodies* (1815).

It should be noted that the Jewish response was not enthusiastic, though it was usually polite. The restorationists were also conversionists, and many saw the two issues as too associated. In addition, many were beginning to believe in emancipation movements and the potential of a good life in the Diaspora. There were exceptions among Jewish people given to more Messianic speculation.

In the United States, these restorationist ideas found committed adherents. In Mordecai Manuel Noah (1785-1851), a Jewish leader was found who believed in cooperation with Gentiles who were for this restoration. Former President John Adams wrote to Noah,

> I really wish the Jews again in Judea, an independent nation, for, as I believe, the most enlightened men of it have participated in the amelioration of the philosophy of the age.

In Noah a voice was raised to the Jewish people of Europe to prepare to return to the land of their ancestors.

All of these trends were building and awaiting a great opportunity. Due to the weakening of the Ottoman Turkish Empire and a temporary revolt under Mohammed Ali, Palestine temporarily came under his rule. England now sought to gain influence and established a British Consulate in Jerusalem, the first in the Land of Israel. It now looked as if the British restoration movement could become a force for real political progress. This movement, as we noted, had its roots in Puritanism and Pietism. Anglicans also were now coming on board.

During this period two parallel movements took place, tying together theological and political dimensions. Edward Bickerstein published an important update of the theology of the restoration movement. It was entitled The Restoration of the Jews to their own Land, in connection with their Future Conversion and the Final Blessedness of the Earth. This book argued for the restoration of the Jewish people to the Land of Israel before their conversion. At this point, Lord Antony Ashley Cooper, the Seventh Earl of Shaftesbury, became committed to the cause. Shaftesbury proposed establishing a colony of the Jews under British protection. The Five Powers, Britain, Austria, Russia, Prussia and Turkey, were in consultation on the Eastern Question and seeking to bring stability to the Middle East. In this Shaftesbury suggested that the five powers commit themselves to the safety of the Jewish people and to fostering the migration of the Jewish people to the Land of Israel. The Foreign Secretary then addressed the British Ambassador in Turkey to strongly recommend to the Turkish Government that they "hold out every encouragement to the Jewish people to return to Palestine."

In Shaftesbury one finds deep pietistic commitments and touching love for Jewish people. Britain could be like Cyrus of old in helping the Jewish people to go back to their land. He spoke of the long ages of the suffering of the Jewish people under the nations. The nations could only make restitution by returning the ancient Land to its ancient people. That it was desolate and unproductive without the Jewish people was used to show the truth of Biblical prophecy. These restorationist ideas were taken up by Charles Henry Churchill, the eldest son of Lord Spencer Churchill. Churchill became British Resident of Damascus and called for a bond between England and the Jewish nation, a hope for their return to the land and the political renewal of Israel as a nation of rank and position among the nations of the earth.

Churchill also sought to influence Western Jewry to take up the cause. Due to the benefits of emancipation, he received a tepid response though Jewish suffering continued in Eastern Europe. The English Jews argued that they could do little unless the Jews of the continent became committed. Unfortunately, the other powers were not so interested; there was no groundswell in the Jewish community, and these efforts came to little. However, it should be noted that this period saw England completely taken by this idea. The press was full of information concerning the ideas of restoration. Churches were a buzz and much literature was produced.

At this time, the connection of the British movement with continental Lutheran Pietism was made. In this case, the idea was that if the Jewish people were to return to the Land then there should again be a movement of believing Jews in the land as part of this fulfillment. What this Jewish movement ought to look like was not carefully considered. Pietist leaders influenced the Prussian King, Frederick William IV, toward the Pietist concern for the Jewish people. He was greatly influenced by Pietist teaching in general. Pietist leaders saw an opportunity to foster the unity of the Church through a unifying project.

These Lutheran Pietists saw it important to establish a Protestant Jewish presence in the Land. Because of their desire for unity, the idea arose to approach Anglican Church leaders. Since the Anglicans believed in apostolic succession, the Lutheran Pietists would be willing to play a supportive role to the project and not the governing role. Eventually Lutheran Pietists in Germany, Norway, Sweden, and Denmark would support this effort in prayer and finances.

The British heard the Pietists. There were presentations to British restorationists and eventually to the Archbishop of Canterbury. Queen Victoria was also approached and supported the idea. This led to legislation in Parliament whereby the Church of England would now seek to establish an Anglican Jewish Bishop in Jerusalem to start a Jewish Protestant movement in the Land. It should be noted that there were always Jewish people in the Land of Israel and in Jerusalem, but the numbers were small.

Michael Solomon Alexander, who had been a Jewish ritual butcher and a reader (Baal Torah), had become a Christian and a strong supporter of the London Society for Promoting Christianity among the Jews. After training he became the first

Evangelical Protestant Bishop of Jerusalem. However, this was not well received by the Jewish people who, though favorable to restorationists who were not placing conversion as a prominent emphasis, were not favorable to a Jewish Christian movement being seen as part of this restoration. Beyond that however, the various Christian groups in the land were not at all happy about the prospects of a Protestant Bishop. Catholic and various Eastern Orthodox leaders made loud protests and provoked an international incident. Turkey appealed to Britain. The upshot was to allow an Anglican Protestant Church, but not a full Bishopric. This church, Christ Church, exists to this day and is just within the Jaffa Gate of the Old City.

Restorationist plans continued to ebb and flow as the 19th century continued. Just a few will be mentioned. Samuel Bradshaw and Thomas Crybaby in Bradshaw's Tract for the times being a plea for the Jews warned Gentiles that it was their duty to aid the liberation of God's ancient people from their depressed and scattered condition by promoting to their utmost their return to the land of their fathers. By this time pogroms had taken place in Russia and Rumania. New efforts for settlement were now taking place. These writers suggested that Turkey give rights to the Land to the Jewish people under Turkish sovereignty while England would also grant safety.

In 1843 Charlotte Elizabeth Browne wrote a novel, Judah's Lion, which is a good source for understanding the general sentiments on restoration. Her hope was for the re-creation of the Church from the Circumcision, which would finally reconcile Judaism and Christianity. The fate of the Jewish people was a common interest at all levels of society, and her book was very popular. Benjamin Disraeli entertained similar hopes to Charlotte Browne as reflected in his novel Tancred. This novel's lead character, Alexander Cohen, dreams of a renewal of Judaism through acceptance of belief in Christ. The effect of the novel was great. Many were now forced to take a position on the issue of Restoration.

In Geneva, Switzerland, Louis Gaussen's Geneva and Jerusalem, picked up on restoration ideas and argued that the restoration of the Jewish people would have utmost importance for the whole civilized world.

A. G. H. Hollingworth called for sending Christian emissaries throughout the world of Jewish communities to convince them of the importance of return to the Land. In 1852, the Association for Promoting Jewish Settlement in Palestine was founded. The Association had a mixed Jewish and Christian committee. John Mills, a Methodist minister, and Sir Hugh William Black were noted Christian members, while Abraham Benisch from Prague was the most prominent Jewish member. Others were Solomon Sequela and Montages. These called for a settlement between Tiberias and Safed.

By mid century, Jewish settlement had begun, amazingly by an American convert to Judaism, James Finn who became the new Consul in Jerusalem. He and his wife were warm friends of the Jewish people. He himself started a settlement and invited Jewish people to cultivate it. He linked the new settlements to the movement in England. A "Society for the Promotion of Jewish Agricultural Labor in the Promised Land" was established as a result. It would link settlements to this group that would continue to foster its expansion. Through Shaftesbury's intercession with British government leaders, the Sultan issued a decree giving a right to settlement to Jewish people. After the Crimean War, Article 9 of the settlement gave Jews rights equal to Christians and a right to settlement.

The Palestine Exploration Fund included some who were committed restorationists. Most noteworthy was Charles Warren who argued that rightly cultivated, and with right industry, the land could support 15 million people! The quest to prove the Bible through archaeology was also connected with deep desires for the fulfillment of prophecy in the land of Israel.

The poetry of Robert Browning included many verses of restoration themes. Browning wrote:

> The Lord will have mercy on Judah yet
> And again in His border see Israel yet,
> When Judah beholds Jerusalem
> The stranger shall be joined to them
> To Jacob's house shall the Gentile cleave
> So the prophet saith and the sons believe

George Elliot's novel *Daniel Deronda* (1886) came at the close of her life. It is an epic of Jewish restoration. Like her fathers and sisters, at a young age she became an Evangelical. Yet as she grew older, the Pietistic Evangelical strain faded. However, these roots influenced an abiding love for the Jewish people and a hope for their restoration rather than assimilation and loss. Elliot's novel had a dramatic effect upon Lithuanian born Yehuda Perlman, who became known as Eliezer Ben Yehuda. The figure of Mordechai in her novel was responsible for his decision to devote his life to the revival of the Hebrew Language in the Land of Israel.

After another war between Russia and Turkey, new hopes for restoration revived. Despite the support of Benjamin Disraeli for a new move for a Jewish Palestine, there was little European support among state leaders and little Jewish enthusiasm. Now events would take place that would lead to more significant settlement. First, Lawrence Oliphant became a great leader in gathering finances and seeking to convince Jewish people of settlement. As a member of Parliament and a London Times correspondent, he reached out to the Jewish people. Though having drifted from more literal Bible doctrine, he saw that funds could be raised to purchase fertile land in Palestine because of the Biblical prophetic hopes that had gained acceptance in so many circles. He received approval to negotiate with Turkey from both Britain and France. He chose land in what is now Jordan and planned to settle and cultivate one and a half million acres with Jewish people from the Pale of Settlement between Russia and Poland (then in Russian control) from Rumania, and from Turkey itself. These would become Turkish citizens, but also have autonomy within the Turkish Empire. However, these plans were thwarted when Gladstone replaced Disraeli and changed policy toward Turkey away from Disraeli's friendship.

The Rumanian and Russian Pogroms (the latter after the assassination of Tsar Alexander II) were extensive and persistent. Many wanted to leave. Tens of thousands came to America. However, among those left a movement for a first Aliyah was taking place. Shaftesbury, at 81, gave himself again to call forth efforts of relief and restoration and joined Oliphant's cause. After providing humanitarian relief efforts and finding a new fervor among the Jewish masses for return to the Land, Oliphant again sought Turkish support but now without a friendship between the two nations of England and Turkey. Settlements were small, and to some discouraging, but Oliphant gave himself to live in the land to encourage them.

Others who also supported the cause of early Zionism in the 1880s were Henry Wentworth Monk and George Nugee. Monk was a devout Christian who assisted Rabbi Sneershon of Jerusalem with the first Jewish settlements. He proposed that Turkey be compensated in cash to give up Palestine for Jewish settlement. Rev. Nugee called for Jewish settlement under British protection.

Rev. William H. Hechler, calling himself a lover of God's ancient people, engaged in intensive activity to collect money for Russian victims of the pogroms and to help them resettle in the Promised Land. He wrote an excellent summary of restoration doctrine and called for Christians to fulfill their role of love in this. He was appointed chaplain of the British embassy in Vienna. Eleven years later he met Theodore Herzl.

American efforts also became important at the end of the nineteenth century. William E. Blackstone, a Methodist minister of Pietist convictions, drafted a petition on March 5, 1891, to President Benjamin Harrison, signed by the Speaker and Clerk of the House of Representatives, the Chairman of the Council of Foreign Affairs, members of Congress, judges, newspaper editors, business and professional leaders, three archbishops, six bishops, 96 other clergymen, and fourteen Rabbis. Many Jewish leaders loved Blackstone though he gave himself to work to convince the Jewish people that Jesus was the promised Messiah. His work was the American Messianic Fellowship in Chicago. His petition supported the Jewish return to settle in Israel and to give international guarantees of safety. Blackstone inherited the basic orientation of the Pietism we have spoken of. He called for the nations to act in the light of the present Jewish suffering. Blackstone wrote:

> The Civilized world says, 'We do not want them,' those who 'are turned back to go -- but where?' One stands appalled before the prospect. It seems as if the agony and horror of 1492 were to be quadrupled in 1892. Will the Christian nations of the nineteenth century stand by the wreck and launch no lifeboat?

He supported the view that the Jewish claim to Palestine had not lapsed. He hoped for an international order, a congress or a court, to settle disputes and that it would recognize Jewish nationhood. How prophetic these words were!

Theodore Herzl finally achieved that success among Jewish people for a restoration of the Jewish people to Israel that had been hoped for by Christian restorationists. Many rabbis and Jewish leaders rejected his plans. Others however, became committed. Rev. William Hechler became the great encourager of Herzl. Here a leading restorationist became the chaplain to the British Embassy in Vienna when the modern Zionist movement was born in that city. Herzl himself knew nothing of the British movement for the restoration of the Jews. Hechler was able to open many state chancelleries to Herzl. The Grand Duke of Baden, a committed Protestant and believer in the restoration (also influenced by Pietist ideas), was informed by Hechler who brought about a meeting with Herzl. He was won for Zionism. This led to Herzl being given audiences with the German Kaiser. Here was then cemented the alliance of political Zionism with the Restoration Movement.

CHAPTER FOUR

THE TWENTIETH CENTURY, ZIONISM AND CHRISTIAN ZIONISTS

Two important British statesmen, Arthur James Balfour, who served as Prime Minister in the days of Herzl's efforts and later as foreign secretary, and David Lloyd George, the future Prime minister became key figures. Both had been influenced by evangelical family roots, in which the restoration of the Jewish people was a fond hope. George's mother and Lady Blanche Balfour were women of profound religious convictions that included belief in the second coming of Jesus and the preceding return of the

Jewish people to the land of Israel. The Isaiah chapters on this return were part of family Bible reading in Balfour's house. Balfour declared in his book *Theism and Humanism* that human history is an instrument for carrying out a Divine purpose. Hence the government of Lloyd George put forth the Balfour declaration, which declared that Palestine was to be the homeland of the Jewish people. Chaim Weizmann was a key in the negotiations that led to the Balfour declaration. Providentially, the events of World War I led to British control of Palestine whereby the gates for immigration could be open. Amazingly, the greatest opposition came from the Board of Deputies of British Jews. However, the groundswell for Zionism was so great that the chairman of the Board was changed to a pro-Zionist. Many were not yet ready for the Zionist idea. Support for the Zionist plan came from President Wilson. Sadly, later British governments bowed to Arab pressures and stemmed the flow of immigration just when it was so needed in the days of Hitler.

In the 1930's a British Major, later to become a General, committed himself to train a Jewish defense force. This famous General, who died in India during World War II, was Orde Wingate. He is credited with the training of the Jewish Army, which later became the

Israel Defense Force. He was a brilliant strategist and totally committed to the Jewish cause. Why? Because of the same Evangelical Pietist roots. He led Jewish forces in self-defense during this period. He grew up in the Plymouth Brethren, a new sect founded by John Nelson Darby in the mid 19th century. This sect taught a glorious future for Israel and was committed to her restoration to the Land of Israel which was common in England at the time of its founding. Wingate would often be seen reading his Bible in times between battles and training sessions. Though eccentric in many ways, his commitment arose from deep religious sentiment. He hoped to be leading the troops when Israel fought and won her full independence.

To this day, Evangelical Pietists in Britain, Scandinavia, South Africa, America, and now in South America are committed to the prosperity and freedom of the Jewish people in the land of Israel and of the Jewish community in the Diaspora as well. It is a doctrinal foundation that is hundreds of years old. Organizations of Evangelicals and Jews have been formed for this purpose, one led by Rabbi Yechiel Eckstein. Denominations have put forth statements in support of Israel as well. The movement for Jewish people in these streams is strong.

CHAPTER FIVE

UNDERSTANDING THE EVANGELICAL PIETIST STREAMS

When we speak of Evangelical Pietism, we are speaking of denominations and movements that have roots in the very Puritan and 17th century Lutheran Pietist and Moravian movements that we described at the beginning of this book. As such, Evangelical Pietists are committed to a deep personal relationship with God through Jesus the Messiah. They believe that the Bible is the Word of God and true in all it teaches (without error). They are often called Bible literalists, and indeed this literalism is the basis for their belief in Israel's glorious future.

However, literalism would be too simplistic a way to describe them, especially the scholars among them. They simply believe that the Bible should be accepted as true in what the Biblical author was asserting. They recognize that there is metaphor, poetry and other kinds of writing in the Bible.

We do not wish to denigrate other religious traditions and recognize the true piety within them, Roman Catholic, Eastern Orthodoxy or other state religious streams. We are glad for any progress that has been made. We are especially pleased with Roman Catholic statements about the Jewish people. The new Catholic Catechism is amazing in this regard. However it is important to distinguish various streams of Christianity. To most Jewish people, all Christianity is the same. Yet Jewish people have only suffered significant persecution under the State churches of the "old world." Roman Catholicism, Eastern Orthodoxy and State Lutheranism are not the same as the Pietist streams. In addition, not all who attach to a religion are real followers of its tenets or in line with its founder.

When we look at the situation in Europe in the days of Hitler, for example, Evangelical Pietism in

Lutheranism was almost dead. The state church was full of the ideas of radical Biblical criticism. Rare were those who believed the Bible as authority as did the Evangelical Pietists of yesteryear. Furthermore, even the Confessing Church Movement did not rediscover and affirm all the tenets of Spenner and Zinzendorf.

Can we distinguish the streams and denominations that are Evangelical Pietist? Yes, there is significant continuity and clarity. The first great movement of Biblical exposition that affirmed a positive Jewish future and called for love toward the Jewish people as chosen of God was the Puritan movement. Some even believed in a restoration to the Land. This greatly set into motion the restorationist movement in England both within and without the Anglican Church, for Puritans were both those who separated and those who remained within. This was a great influence on the Lutheran Pietists in Germany and then in the Scandinavian nations. (Pietism is still strong in Scandinavia within the Lutheran Church.) Such people stood for civil rights for the Jewish people and for loving relationships with them. The Moravian movement of Zinzendorf spread these ideas far and wide. These Pietist ideas continued to have influence in the Evangelical branch of Anglicanism.

The next great Pietist movement was the Methodist movement. As we saw, the Wesleys supported Israel's restoration. After John Wesley's death, Methodism was not just a Pietist movement within Anglicanism as Spenner's Pietism had been within Lutheranism. It became a new denomination that in the United States was to become, for a time, the largest Protestant denomination. Lutheran Pietism remained strong in Scandinavia and had some influence on favorable treatment of the Jewish people during World War II. Indeed, the Danish rescue of the Jewish population was probably rooted in such sentiments. Free Churches that left the State controlled churches carried with them the Pietist ideas concerning Israel. Indeed, we see this in the Evangelical Free Church in America, which has passed beyond its Scandinavian roots and produced one of America's largest and most respected seminaries, Trinity Evangelical Divinity School. This denomination is very pro-Israel and serves many denominations. Former Deans Kenneth Kantzer and Walter Kaiser are known for their support for the Jewish people. The former President of this Church body, Arnold Olsen, was a great supporter of Israel.

However, many denominations and streams were birthed in America. The holiness movement in the

19th century was Methodist rooted and a return to a rejuvenation of Pietist principles. A faith in the future of Israel and her prophetic destiny was part of the mix. From this holiness movement, camps, revivals, Keswick conferences, etc. came many new denominations. The Nazarene denomination; the Christian and Missionary Alliance; the Assembly of God; the Church of God, Cleveland; the Pentecostal Holiness denomination; and others stem from these days. In addition, the Dallas Seminary orbit of churches that traces to J. N. Darby maintains a staunch stand of pro-Israel Zionism. New steams of churches that are birthed out of these are also maintaining Zionist commitments. However, where Biblical authority fades, as in the largest Methodist denomination and in the American Episcopal Church, while there is a praiseworthy stance against anti-Semitism, there is a loss of a prophetic commitment to Israel. Liberal criticism removes the literal interpretation of prophecy in which Christian Zionist convictions flourish. The Southern Baptist denomination, which is now the largest Protestant denomination in the United States, traces its roots to the Puritans in the 17th century. Their stance on Israel was influenced by the Puritanism of the time and by later Pietist influences. One would clearly say that the stance of the Southern Baptists is the stance of Evangelical Pietism. Space does not allow us to mention all the Evangelical leaders and groups that have continued the same stance on Israel to this day. Many denominations have put out Israel and Jewish support statements. Such a leader as the late Arnold Olsen, who traveled countless times to Israel, is one example. Southern Baptist Billy Graham has been a consistent leader for the whole Evangelical world in this regard. John Hagee from Houston is another such national leader as is John McArthur in California. Jack Hayford has become well known for his support for Israel and the Jewish community. We also well mention Clarence Wagner of Bridges for Peace. There is the late Dr. David Lewis of Christians United for Israel, who has given himself in great persistence in organizational leadership, newspaper publishing, and Israel tours to foster continued pro-Jewish and pro-Israel commitments in the Evangelical community. George Morrison in Denver has become a national leader among Evangelicals for Israel and the Jewish community. The pastor of the largest church in the world, Dr. David Yonggi Cho, in Seoul, Korea is from an Assembly of God background. He is committed to supporting the Jewish people and Israel. So the tradition of Evangelical Pietism with regard to Israel and the Jewish people remains strong. This support was not as clear after World War II because many denominations were becoming liberal and giving up Evangelical convictions. The Evangelical Pietists were a minority of American Protestants. However, this is no longer the case. They are the majority Protestant movement.

To my knowledge there has never been a call for Jewish persecution or rejection of the Jewish people from any Evangelical Pietist group. This is an amazing history of 400 years in continuity, and the Jewish community knows almost nothing of it. It is even more significant in the light of the fact that liberal Judaism opposes the social policy ideas of most of these Christians. This great history is lost in the smoke and fire of persecutions and actions taken in state church situations. This does not mean that there are not Evangelicals that are prejudiced or hold uneducated ideas about Judaism and the Jews. There are some who are replacement in theology. However, only a very small minority is replacement, though I am sad to say it is a growing minority today. With regard to anti-Semitism, it is generally an individual matter and mostly an educational-discipleship concern. In addition, Evangelical Pietism has generally supported a moderate understanding of separation of church and state. In this they mean that the State should acknowledge God and be accountable to Him for its sphere, but no one religious body should be favored. However, religious tolerance does not extend to practices in the society that destroy the moral foundations of family, integrity, honesty and the general understanding known as the Judeo-Christian ethic. That ethic should be acknowledged as the foundation of society and its laws. We can see that we cannot treat all religions equally when we remember that some religions practice human sacrifice!

One would expect that the greatest friendship would thus develop between the Jewish community and the Evangelical Pietist community. However, there are several areas of strain. One is the issue of Church and State. The Jewish community (not the Orthodox Jewish community) supports a radical separation of Church and State whereby the State is no longer accountable to God. Evangelical Pietists see this as causing the State is to accept an excessive tolerance and even support for behavior that is destructive to society. Evangelicals also fear that this can lead the State to claim ultimate authority and yield to tyranny. However, the Jewish community often sees the Evangelical Pietist stand as leading to a theocracy ruled by Christian Churches. This is not what Evangelical Pietists seek. They seek more of the stable moral order of the nation's first 175 years. The issue is not aided by the lack of clear thinking by some Evangelical Pietists who speak out socially and politically. At any rate, this produces a tension, but one where the Evangelical Pietists have still maintained support for the Jewish people, though disagreeing on these issues. One would find men such as Rabbi Daniel Lapin and Dennis Prager agreeing more with the Evangelical positions.

The second area of tension is that Evangelical Pietists would like to see the Jewish people believe that Jesus is the Messiah. Some of these hold to what is called the wider hope view and believe that people who respond to natural revelation, and especially Jewish people who respond to the Hebrew Bible, can be saved through the atonement of Jesus. However, others believe that those who do not accept Jesus as Lord and Messiah before they die will go to Hell. This is extremely repugnant to Jewish people of all stripes. Some have even called it hate speech. Responding to this is most difficult. How can we respond?

Evangelical Pietists are motivated to share the Gospel with all people that they might come into the abundant life of faith in Jesus. They also are motivated by love to prevent such a sad ending of judgment and Hell. While Jewish leaders have seen such a doctrine as hatred and even hate speech, one must understand that it is neither hate speech nor prejudice from within the Evangelical framework. Indeed, though they may not like this doctrine, Evangelicals generally believe they are forced to this conclusion by what the Bible teaches. This does not mean that they hate those who do not become believers in Jesus. Indeed, churches constantly exhort their members that they must love the unconverted all the more, for only so will the greatest number be saved. It is not ethnic or racial prejudice, for the Evangelical teaches that all are in the same boat. All are lost; no one's works measure up to attain salvation, so one must receive an imparted righteousness that only comes by faith in the atonement of Jesus. This is a fully egalitarian doctrine though it is hard. In a day of religious relativism, it seems unbelievably narrow, but Evangelical Pietists believe they have found the truth. They are not relativists, but believe in absolutes. The same literal approach to the Bible that leads them to such a stark view of Heaven and Hell, leads them to an absolute commitment to the Jewish people and Israel as God's chosen. There are some who believe that the issue of Heaven and Hell in context is not so simple. They are a significant minority.

In this regard Evangelical Pietists hope for Jewish people to believe some day. Some see this as only happening at the end of this Age when the Messiah comes. They make no effort to convert Jews. Some believe that the Jewish people are the one exception and may be saved through their covenant relationship with God without accepting Jesus in this life, though his atonement is the reason for the acceptance. (There are many statements in classical Jewish literature that state that all idolaters, who comprise most of the world historically, are lost.) However, most, though they may not voice it, believe that Jewish people need Jesus just like everyone else. This produces great tension for Jewish people who believe that accepting Jesus would lead to assimilation and the end of the Jewish people, a spiritual holocaust. Some Evangelical Pietists have not thought through the implications. However, others hearken back to a few of the earlier Pietist and Puritan thinkers who thought there could be a Jewish expression of New Testament truth whereby Jewish life and culture based in Torah would be preserved. In this regard, some see the Messianic Jewish movement of Jews who accept Jesus (whom they call Yeshua), form congregations and live a Jewish life as being a good thing and a solution to the problem of Jesus and assimilation. Was not this the example and teaching of the Apostles, the disciples of Jesus? The Jewish community wants Evangelicals to reject the Messianic Jews as a prerequisite for good relationships with the mainstream Jewish community. The Evangelicals say how can we reject our brothers and sisters who share our faith in Jesus?

What is to be done? Well, first of all, let each group really understand where they are coming from without misrepresenting the other. Second, it is often said by Jewish leaders that the Evangelical support for the Jews is shallow, and when they do not convert or prophecy ideas about Israel do not fit fully, they will be abandoned and turned on. The doctrine of Heaven and Hell is seen as leading to this conclusion. How can you think well of someone whom you think is lost and going to Hell? Yet, this has not been a problem throughout the 400-year history we have been describing. It is an amazing fact that the Evangelical Pietist Christians, who have believed in a stark doctrine of Heaven and Hell from the Puritans on, have been the best supporters of the Jews. Cromwell so believed and fought for the opening of England to the Jews. So did many of the others written about in this book. Evangelicals would say that they love others because, though the image of God has been marred, every person is still sacred and in the image of God and deserves unconditional love. This does not mean that there is not to be justice for crimes in society, but there is always a desire for the guilty to repent and be saved until the last breath. One sees worth and goodness in the image of God in every human being though not sufficient for salvation; for God requires a perfection that is only in Jesus. Finally, though Luther changed in his regard for the Jewish people, this is not true in the history of Evangelical Pietism, which began among Puritans one hundred years after Luther's reformation.

Evangelical Pietists do not expect the great mass of Jews to become believers in Jesus until He returns. Until then, they want to be supportive of both the Jewish community and the small minority of Jews who follow Jesus Since Jewish people as a whole are not expected to believe until the coming of the Messiah at the end of this Age, that Jewish people do not believe in him does not dampen zeal or love for them. It is a doctrinal conviction that followers of Jesus are to love, show mercy, stand with and support the Jewish people and fight anti-Semitism. Luther turned, but does anyone have any examples of Evangelical Pietists who first professed love for the Jewish people and then turned on them? Kobler's book gives massive documentation with no instance of an Evangelical Pietist who turned against the Jewish people. Luther cannot be considered a pattern in any way for the Pietist response to the Jewish people.

So we come to paradoxes and some recommendations. First of all, many would like to see the Jewish community believe in Jesus but do not expect that most will do so until Jesus comes. Second, many of these same folks believe that faith in Jesus is necessary for salvation. Third, these same folks believe they are duty bound to love and support the Jews until the Messiah comes. They follow an absolute ethic of right and wrong. Here is the paradox, one seen by Dennis Prager but missed by many others. The Jewish community has flourished in America largely because of the brand of Christianity in America. If Prager were to delve deeper, he would call this brand Evangelical Pietism. Prager sees that Jewish people are safer in an environment where such Christianity is strong than in an environment where relativism and atheism prevail. Prager is a wise Rabbi and radio personality in Los Angeles. One sees that in the loss of God and absolutes, anything is possible. Good can be called evil and evil good. So Prager hopes that American

Evangelicalism flourishes and becomes stronger and more influential. Looking at Communism and other relativistic philosophies is much scarier.

In this, I recommend that Evangelical Pietists and Jews form bonds of mutual love and cooperation. There is common ground for which they can work. In this mutual love and respect, both will have to put up with views that are repugnant to the other. It would be well, however, to accurately understand these views and not a caricature of them. Jewish people can educate their people to seek to prevent them from becoming followers of Jesus and to say no to the invitation to faith given by Evangelical Pietists and Messianic Jews. Traditional Jewish people can share their faith as well. After all, more Gentiles are becoming Jewish than Jewish people are becoming followers of Jesus. Evangelical Pietists stand ready to repent for all negative attitudes and stereotypes among their people. In addition, they are repentant for the history of Christianity; for before Puritans and Evangelicals, the Catholic, Eastern Churches, and Lutheran state churches were "the Church." So they are repentant for the history that took place under state churches. No, Evangelical Christians will not repudiate Messianic Jews (though they may sometimes be quiet about their beliefs about them for good relationship's sake). Messianic Jews will continue to argue that Christian Zionists should include them in their prayers and support. They will assert that they are the heirs of the apostolic Messianic Jewish communities of the first century and have a special claim of love from the larger Christian community. This is a strong argument that will convince many Christians. Non-Orthodox Jews will not soon abandon political liberalism and other views Evangelicals find troubling. However, in support for a strong Israel, compassion for the poor and needy who should be served by church and synagogue, in fighting hatred and prejudice, Jews and Christians can make common cause to the betterment of all. The history of Evangelical Pietism and the Jewish people proves that this is not only possible, but has happened in ways that have greatly benefited the Jewish community. Indeed, when Evangelical Pietism prevails in a society, the Jewish people are favored and flourish. This is the opposite of what many Jews believe, but it is true. This book tells a story about streams in Christianity that have been consistently pro-Jewish. It is an encouraging story.

Annotated Bibliography

Bierman, John and Colin Smith. *Fire in the Night: Wingate of Burma, Ethiopia, and Zion* (New York: Random House, 1999). This very stimulating biography presents the Christian Zionist roots of the man who is credited with establishing the Israel Defense Force in its earlier state before World War II.

Crombie, Kevin. *For the Love of Zion, Christian Witness and the Restoration of Israel* (Hodder and Stoughton, 1991). Crombie provides several quotes from some of the same authors used in discussing this history. It tells a similar story to this book, but is not as comprehensive describing some of the key figures in theology and exegesis since the Reformation. Some were clear on the continued election of Israel and others as noted in our book did see the restoration to the Land. A few other theologians and exegetes are noted, but very important ones.

Kjaer-Hansen, Kai. *Joseph Rabinowitz and The Messianic Movement*, published by Eerdmans, Grand Rapids, Michigan in 1995, has also informed me. Also, note that there have been several good articles in *Mishkan*, published in Jerusalem, with many writings being of today's Lutheran Pietist convictions.

Kobler, Franz. *The Vision Was There* (London: World Jewish Congress, 1954). This amazing book gives the full bibliographical information on most of the out of print books on Christian commitment to Jewish restoration quoted in the text. Finding the book in old libraries in England or Scotland is possible, but Kobler, amazingly did the travel and research.

Loden, Lisa. *The Land Cries Out* (Eugene, Oregon: Wipf and Stock, 2011). The book provides important essays by scholars who are in agreement with the restoration of Israel and the exegesis that supports it. They quote some of our historic names. The book includes those who have a case against the restoration of Israel views. One writer, Colin Chapman, actually notes the restorationists, going back to the Puritans, but then rejects their views. He seems to be saying that this was a small stream of leaders and exegetes, but then goes on to try to refute the views.

Murray, Ian. *The Puritan Hope* (London: Banner of Truth, 1992. This book has the best presentation on Puritan eschatology that I have ever seen. The sections on the salvation of Israel provide many of the primary references that are noted in the book.

Murray, John. *The Epistle to the Romans* (Grand Rapids, Michigan: Eerdmans, 1997, a reprint of the classic from the 1960s). The book has an excellent exegesis of Romans 11 that refutes replacement theology. This is important because he is a classic Reformed thinker.

Prince, Derek. *Our Debt to Israel* (Derek Prince Ministries: Charlotte, North Carolina, 2008, an update of an earlier volume). This short but good read also uses Franz Kobler's book to refer to classic sources.

Skarsaune, Oscar. *Israel's Friend* (Oslo, 1994). This is only in Norwegian, but tells the wonderful story of the Pietist influence in Scandinavia. I was able to understand the content of this book by sitting with Professor Skarsaune in his office in Oslo, Norway. The history of the relationship of the Puritans to the German and Scandinavians Pietists, and then the Moravians is excellent. Then Skarsaune gives information up to the Lutheran cooperation with the British Anglicans on the founding of Christ Church led by Jewish Bishop Solomon Alexander.

Weinlick, John R. *Count Zinzendorf: The Story of His Life and Leadership in the Renewed Moravian Church* (Bethlehem, Pennsylvania: Moravian Publishing, 1984). This classic biography has important information.

About Dan Juster
and Tikkun Ministries

Dr. Daniel Juster is the Director of Tikkun International, a network of congregations and ministries in the United States and abroad. He was an honors graduate in philosophy from Wheaton College, completed graduate course work for a degree in Philosophy of Religion at Trinity Evangelical Seminary, and received a Masters of Divinity from McCormick Theological Seminary. He also received a Th.D. from New Covenant International Seminary, New Zealand.

Founding president of the Union of Messianic Jewish Congregations, which he served as president and general secretary, he also pastored congregations Adat Hatikvah in

Chicago and later Beth Messiah in suburban Washington, D.C. from 1978-2000. In recent years, he and his wife Patty have resided near Jerusalem.

Dr. Juster is an author of several books on Messianic Jewish theology and apologetics. He serves on numerous boards to further the Messianic Jewish movement's relationship with the Church.

Tikkun International is the U.S. agency for Revive Israel and Ohalai Rachamim, which are planting, discipleship, and networking ministries in Israel. Tikkun also provides oversight of the international teaching and networking ministry of Dr. Juster. Tikkun America, a part of Tikkun International, links a network of Messianic Jewish Congregations in North America.

His ministry may be contacted at
www.Tikkunministries.org,
or by writing Tikkun@tikkunministries.org.

Other Related Resources

Available at Messianic Jewish Resources Int'l. • www.messianicjewish.net
1-800-410-7367
(Prices subject to change.)

Complete Jewish Bible: *A New English Version*
—Dr. David H. Stern

Presenting the Word of God as a unified Jewish book, the *Complete Jewish Bible* is a new version for Jews and non-Jews alike. It connects Jews with the Jewishness of the Messiah, and non-Jews with their Jewish roots. Names and key terms are returned to their original Hebrew and presented in easy-to-understand transliterations, enabling the reader to say them the way Yeshua (Jesus) did! 1697 pages.

Hardback	9789653590151	JB12	$34.99
Paperback	9789653590182	JB13	$29.99
Leather Cover	9789653590199	JB15	$59.99
Large Print (12 Pt font)	9781880226483	JB16	$49.99

Jewish New Testament
—Dr. David H. Stern

The New Testament is a Jewish book, written by Jews, initially for Jews. Its central figure was a Jew. His followers were all Jews; yet no other version really communicates its original, essential Jewishness. Uses neutral terms and Hebrew names. Highlights Jewish references and corrects mistranslations. Freshly translated into English from Greek, this is a must read to learn about first-century faith. 436 pages

Hardback	9789653590069	JB02	$19.99
Paperback	9789653590038	JB01	$14.99
MP3	9781880226575	JC02	$49.99
20 CD's	9781880226384	JC01	$49.99

Jewish New Testament Commentary
—Dr. David H. Stern

This companion to the *Jewish New Testament* enhances Bible study. Passages and expressions are explained in their original cultural context. 15 years of research. 960 pages.

Hardback	9789653590083	JB06	$34.99
Paperback	9789653590113	JB10	$29.99

Jewish New Testament on CD

All the richness of the *Jewish New Testament* beautifully narrated in English by professional narrator/singer, Jonathan Settel. Thrilling to hear, you will enjoy listening to the Hebrew names, expressions and locations as spoken by Messiah.

20 CDs	9781880226384	JC01	$49.99

Jewish New Testament & Commentary on CD-ROM

Do word searches, studies and more! And, because this is part of the popular LOGOS Bible program, you will have the "engine" to access one of the top Bible research systems. As an option, you'll be able to obtain and cross reference the Mishnah, Josephus, Bible dictionaries, and much more! Windows 3.1+ only.

| | 9789653590120 | JCD02 | $39.99 |

Messianic Judaism *A Modern Movement With an Ancient Past*
—David H. Stern

An updated discussion of the history, ideology, theology and program for Messianic Judaism. A challenge to both Jews and non-Jews who honor Yeshua to catch the vision of Messianic Judaism. 312 pages

| | 9781880226339 | LB62 | $17.99 |

Restoring the Jewishness of the Gospel
A Message for Christians
—David H. Stern

Introduces Christians to the Jewish roots of their faith, challenges some conventional ideas, and raises some neglected questions: How are both the Jews and "the Church" God's people? Is the Law of Moses in force today? Filled with insight! Endorsed by Dr. Darrell L. Bock. 110 pages

| English | 9781880226667 | LB70 | $9.99 |
| Spanish | 9789653590175 | JB14 | $9.99 |

Yeshua *A Guide to the Real Jesus and the Original Church*
—Dr. Ron Moseley

Opens up the history of the Jewish roots of the Christian faith. Illuminates the Jewish background of Yeshua and the Church and never flinches from showing "Jesus was a Jew, who was born, lived, and died, within first century Judaism." Explains idioms in the New Testament. Endorsed by Dr. Brad Young and Dr. Marvin Wilson. 213 pages.

| | 9781880226681 | LB29 | $12.99 |

The Irrevocable Calling *Israel's Role As A Light To The Nations*
—Daniel C. Juster, Th.D.

Referring to the chosen-ness of the Jewish people, Paul, the Apostle, wrote "For God's free gifts and his calling are irrevocable" (Rom. 11:29). This messenger to the Gentiles understood the unique calling of his people, Israel. So does Dr. Daniel Juster, President of Tikkun Ministries Int'l. In *The Irrevocable Calling*, he expands Paul's words, showing how Israel was uniquely chosen to bless the world and how these blessings can be enjoyed today. Endorsed by Dr. Jack Hayford, Mike Bickle and Don Finto. 64 pages.

| | 9781880226346 | LB66 | $8.99 |

Gateways to Torah *Joining the Ancient Conversation on the Weekly Portion*
—Rabbi Russell Resnik

From before the days of Messiah until today, Jewish people have read from and discussed a prescribed portion of the Pentateuch each week. Now, a Messianic Jewish Rabbi, Russell Resnik, brings another perspective on the Torah, that of a Messianic Jew. 246 pages.

9781880226889   **LB42** $15.99

Creation to Completion *A Guide to Life's Journey from the Five Books of Moses*
—Rabbi Russell Resnik

Endorsed by Coach Bill McCartney, Founder of Promise Keepers & Road to Jerusalem: "Paul urged Timothy to study the Scriptures (2 Tim. 3:16), advising him to apply its teachings to all aspects of his life. Since there was no New Testament then, this rabbi/apostle was convinced that his disciple would profit from studying the Torah, the Five Books of Moses, and the Old Testament. Now, Rabbi Resnik has written a warm devotional commentary that will help you understand and apply the Law of Moses to your life in a practical way." 256 pages

9781880226322   **LK48** $14.99

Walk Genesis!   Walk Exodus!   Walk Leviticus!   Walk Numbers!   Walk Deuteronomy!
Messianic Jewish Devotional Commentaries
—Jeffrey Enoch Feinberg, Ph.D.

Using the weekly synagogue readings, Dr. Jeff rey Feinberg has put together some very valuable material in his "Walk" series. Each section includes a short Hebrew lesson (for the non-Hebrew speaker), key concepts, an excellent overview of the portion, and some practical applications. Can be used as a daily devotional as well as a Bible study tool.

Walk Genesis!	238 pages	9781880226759	**LB34**	$12.99
Walk Exodus!	224 pages	9781880226926	**LB40**	$12.99
Walk Leviticus!	208 pages	9781880226186	**LB45**	$12.99
Walk Numbers!	211 pages	9781880226872	**LB48**	$12.99
Walk Deuteronomy!	231 pages	9781880226995	**LB51**	$12.99
SPECIAL! Five-book Walk!	5 Book Set	**Save $10**	**LK28**	$54.99

Classes by Netzer David International Yeshiva on CD for personal or group study!
Hear awesome teaching from Dr. John Fischer, Th.D, Ph.D.

The Gospels in their Jewish Context

An examination of the Jewish background and nature of the Gospels in their contemporary political, cultural and historical settings, emphasizing each gospel's special literary presentation of Yeshua, and highlighting the cultural and religious contexts necessary for understanding each of the gospels. 32 Hours of Instruction and pdf of Syllabus.

LCD01 $49.99

The Epistles from a Jewish Perspective

An examination of the relationship of Rabbi Shaul (the Apostle Paul) and the Apostles to their Jewish contemporaries and environment; surveys their Jewish practices, teaching, controversy with the religious leaders, and many critical passages, with emphasis on the Jewish nature, content, and background of these letters. 32 Hours of Instruction and pdf of Syllabus.

LCD02 $49.99

They Loved the Torah *What Yeshua's First Followers Really Thought About the Law*
—Dr. David Friedman

Although many Jews believe that Paul taught against the Law, this book disproves that notion. An excellent case for his premise that all the fi rst followers of the Messiah were not only Torah-observant, but also desired to spread their love for God's entire Word to the gentiles to whom they preached. 144 pages. Endorsed by Dr. David Stern, Ariel Berkowitz, Rabbi Dr. Stuart Dauermann & Dr. John Fischer.

9781880226940   **LB47** $9.99

The Distortion *2000 Years of Misrepresenting the Relationship Between Jesus the Messiah and the Jewish People*
—Dr. John Fischer & Dr. Patrice Fischer

Did the Jews kill Jesus? Did they really reject him? With the rise of global anti–Semitism, it is important to understand what the Gospels teach about the relationship between Jewish people and their Messiah. 2000 years of distortion have made this diffi cult. Learn how the distortion began and continues to this day and what you can do to change it. 126 pages. Endorsed by Dr. Ruth Fleischer, Rabbi Russell Resnik, Dr. Daniel C. Juster, Dr. Michael Rydelnik.

9781880226254   **LB54** $11.99

God's Appointed Times *A Practical Guide to Understanding and Celebrating the Biblical Holidays – New Edition.*
—Barney Kasdan

The Biblical Holy Days teach us about the nature of God and his plan for mankind, and can be a source of God's blessing for all believers–Jews and Gentiles–today. Includes historical background, traditional Jewish observance, New Testament relevance, and prophetic significance, plus music, crafts and holiday recipes. 145 pages.

English	9781880226353	LB63	$12.99
Spanish	9781880226551	LB59	$12.99

God's Appointed Customs *A Messianic Jewish Guide to the Biblical Lifecycle and Lifestyle*
—Barney Kasdan

Explains how biblical customs are often the missing key to unlocking the depths of Scripture. Discusses circumcision, the Jewish wedding, and many more customs mentioned in the New Testament. Companion to *God's Appointed Times.* 170 pages.

English	9781880226636	LB26	$12.99
Spanish	9781880226391	LB60	$12.99

Celebrations of the Bible *A Messianic Children's Curriculum*

Did you know that each Old Testament feast or festival finds its fulfillment in the New? They enrich the lives of people who experience and enjoy them. Our popular curriculum for children is in a brand new, user-friendly format. The lay-flat at binding allows you to easily reproduce handouts and worksheets. Celebrations of the Bible has been used by congregations, Sunday schools, ministries, homeschoolers, and individuals to teach children about the biblical festivals. Each of these holidays are presented for Preschool (2-K), Primary (Grades 1-3), Junior (Grades 4-6), and Children's Worship/Special Services. 208 pages.

9781880226261	LB55	$24.99

Passover: *The Key That Unlocks the Book of Revelation*
—Daniel C. Juster, Th.D.

Is there any more enigmatic book of the Bible than Revelation? Controversy concerning its meaning has surrounded it back to the first century. Today, the arguments continue. Yet, Dan Juster has given us the key that unlocks the entire book—the events and circumstances of the Passover/Exodus.
By interpreting Revelation through the lens of Exodus, Dan Juster provides a unified overview that helps us read Revelation as it was always meant to be read, as a drama of spiritual conflict, deliverance, and above all, worship. He also shows how this final drama, fulfilled in Messiah, resonates with the Torah and all of God's Word. — Russ Resnik, Executive Director • Union of Messianic Jewish Congregations. 144 Pages.

9781936716210	LB74	$10.99

The Messianic Passover Haggadah
Revised and Updated

Guides you through the traditional Passover seder dinner, step-by-step. Not only does this observance remind us of our rescue from Egyptian bondage, but, we remember Messiah's last supper, a Passover seder. The theme of redemption is seen throughout the evening. What's so unique about our Haggadah is the focus on Yeshua (Jesus) the Messiah and his teaching, especially on his last night in the upper room. 36 pages.

English	9781880226292	LB57	$4.99
Spanish	9781880226599	LBSP01	$4.99

The Messianic Passover Seder Preparation Guide

Includes recipes, blessings and songs. 19 pages.

English	9781880226247	LB10	$2.99
Spanish	9781880226728	LBSP02	$2.99

The Sabbath *Entering God's Rest*
—Barry Rubin & Steffi Rubin

Even if you've never celebrated Shabbat before, this book will guide you into the rest God has for all who would enter in—Jews and non-Jews. Contains prayers, music, recipes; in short, everything you need to enjoy the Sabbath, even how to observe havdalah, the closing ceremony of the Sabbath. Also discusses the Saturday or Sunday controversy. 48 pages.

9781880226742	LB32	$6.99

Havdalah *The Ceremony that Completes the Sabbath*
—Dr. Neal & Jamie Lash

The Sabbath ends with this short, yet equally sweet ceremony called havdalah (separation). This ceremony reminds us to be a light and a sweet fragrance in this world of darkness as we carry the peace, rest, joy and love of the Sabbath into the work week. 28 pages.

9781880226605	LB69	$4.99

Dedicate and Celebrate!
A Messianic Jewish Guide to Hanukkah
—Barry Rubin & Family

Hanukkah means "dedication" — a theme of significance for Jews and Christians. Discussing its historical background, its modern-day customs, deep meaning for all of God's people, this little book covers all the how-tos! Recipes, music, and prayers for lighting the menorah, all included! 32 pages.

9781880226834	LB36	$4.99

The Conversation
An Intimate Journal of the Emmaus Encounter
—Judy Salisbury

"Then beginning with Moses and with all the prophets, He explained to them the things concerning Himself in all the Scriptures." Luke 24:27
If you've ever wondered what that conversation must have been like, this captivating book takes you there.
"The Conversation brings to life that famous encounter between the two disciples and our Lord Jesus on the road to Emmaus. While it is based in part on an imaginative reconstruction, it is filled with the throbbing pulse of the excitement of the sensational impact that our Lord's resurrection should have on all of our lives." ~ Dr. Walter Kaiser President Emeritus Gordon-Conwell Theological Seminary. Hardcover 120 pages.

9781936716173   **LB73** $14.99

Growing to Maturity
A Messianic Jewish Discipleship Guide
—Daniel C. Juster, Th.D.

This discipleship series presents first steps of understanding and spiritual practice, tailored for the Jewish believer. It's purpose is to aid the believer in living according to Yeshua's will as a disciple, one who has learned the example of his teacher. The course is structured according to recent advances in individualized educational instruction. Discipleship is serious business and the material is geared for serious study and reflection. Each chapter is divided into short sections followed by study questions. 256 pages.

9781936716227   **TB15** $19.99

Growing to Maturity Primer: *A Messianic Jewish Discipleship Workbook*
—Daniel C. Juster, Th.D.

A basic book of material in question and answer form. Usable by everyone. 60 pages.

9780961455507   **TB16** $7.99

Proverbial Wisdom & Common Sense
—Derek Leman

A Messianic Jewish Approach to Today's Issues from the Proverbs Unique in style and scope, this commentary on the book of Proverbs, written in devotional style, is divided into chapters suitable for daily reading. A virtual encyclopedia of practical advice on family, sex, fi nances, gossip, honesty, love, humility, and discipline. Endorsed by Dr. John Walton, Dr. Jeff rey Feinberg and Rabbi Barney Kasdan. 248 pages.

9781880226780   **LB35** $14.99

That They May Be One *A Brief Review of Church Restoration Movements and Their Connection to the Jewish People*
—Daniel Juster, Th.D

Something prophetic and momentous is happening. The Church is finally fully grasping its relationship to Israel and the Jewish people. Author describes the restoration movements in Church history and how they connected to Israel and the Jewish people. Each one contributed in some way—some more, some less—toward the ultimate unity between Jews and Gentiles. Predicted in the Old Testament and fulfilled in the New, Juster believes this plan of God finds its full expression in Messianic Judaism. He may be right. See what you think as you read *That They May Be One*. 100 pages.

9781880226711	**LB71**	$9.99

The Greatest Commandment
How the Sh'ma Leads to More Love in Your Life
—Irene Lipson

"What is the greatest commandment?" Yeshua was asked. His reply—"Hear, O Israel, the Lord our God, the Lord is one, and you are to love Adonai your God with all your heart, with all your soul, with all your understanding, and all your strength." A superb book explaining each word so the meaning can be fully grasped and lived. Endorsed by Elliot Klayman, Susan Perlman, & Robert Stearns. 175 pages.

9781880226360	**LB65**	$12.99

Blessing the King of the Universe
Transforming Your Life Through the Practice of Biblical Praise
—Irene Lipson

Insights into the ancient biblical practice of blessing God are offered clearly and practically. With examples from Scripture and Jewish tradition, this book teaches the biblical formula used by men and women of the Bible, including the Messiah; points to new ways and reasons to praise the Lord; and explains more about the Jewish roots of the faith. Endorsed by Rabbi Barney Kasdan, Dr. Mitch Glaser, & Rabbi Dr. Dan Cohn-Sherbok. 144 pages.

9781880226797	**LB53**	$11.99

You Bring the Bagels, I'll Bring the Gospel
Sharing the Messiah with Your Jewish Neighbor
Revised Edition—Now with Study Questions
—Rabbi Barry Rubin

This "how-to-witness-to-Jewish-people" book is an orderly presentation of everything you need to share the Messiah with a Jewish friend. Includes Messianic prophecies, Jewish objections to believing, sensitivities in your witness, words to avoid. A "must read" for all who care about the Jewish people. Good for individual or group study. Used in Bible schools. Endorsed by Harold A. Sevener, Dr. Walter C. Kaiser, Dr. Erwin J. Kolb and Dr. Arthur F. Glasser. 253 pages.

English		**9781880226650** **LB13**	$12.99
Te Tengo Buenas Noticias	**9780829724103**	**OBSP02**	$14.99

Making Eye Contact With God
A Weekly Devotional for Women
—Terri Gillespie

What kind of eyes do you have? Are they downcast and sad? Are they full of God's joy and passion? See yourself through the eyes of God. Using real life anecdotes, combined with scripture, the author reveals God's heart for women everywhere, as she softly speaks of the ways in which women see God. Endorsed by prominent authors: Dr. Angela Hunt, Wanda Dyson and Kathryn Mackel. 247 pages, hardcover.

9781880226513   **LB68** $19.99

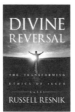

Divine Reversal
The Transforming Ethics of Jesus
—Rabbi Russell Resnik

In the Old Testament, God often reversed the plans of man. Yeshua's ethics continue this theme. Following his path transforms one's life from within, revealing the source of true happiness, forgiveness, reconciliation, fidelity and love. From the introduction, "As a Jewish teacher, Jesus doesn't separate matters of theology from practice. His teaching is consistently practical, ethical, and applicable to real life, even two thousand years after it was originally given." Endorsed by Jonathan Bernis, Dr. Daniel C. Juster, Dr. Jeffrey L. Seif, and Dr Darrell Bock. 206 pages

9781880226803   **LB72** $12.99

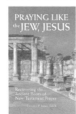

Praying Like the Jew, Jesus
Recovering the Ancient Roots of New Testament Prayer
—Dr. Timothy P. Jones

This eye-opening book reveals the Jewish background of many of Yeshua's prayers. Historical vignettes "transport" you to the times of Yeshua so you can grasp the full meaning of Messiah's prayers. Unique devotional thoughts and meditations, presented in down-to-earth language, provide inspiration for a more meaningful prayer life and help you draw closer to God. Endorsed by Mark Galli, James W. Goll, Rev. Robert Stearns, James F. Strange, and Dr. John Fischer. 144 pages.

9781880226285   **LB56** $9.99

Growing Your Olive Tree Marriage A Guide for Couples
from Two Traditions
—David J. Rudolph

One partner is Jewish; the other is Christian. Do they celebrate Hanukkah, Christmas or both? Do they worship in a church or a synagogue? How will the children be raised? This is the fi rst book from a biblical perspective that addresses the concerns of intermarried couples, off ering a godly solution. Includes highlights of interviews with intermarried couples. Endorsed by Walter C. Kaiser, Jr., Rabbi Dan Cohn-Sherbok, Jonathan Settel, Dr. Mitchell Glaser & Natalie Sirota. 224 pages.

9781880226179   **LB50** $12.99

In Search of the Silver Lining *Where is God in the Midst of Life's Storms?*
—Jerry Gramckow
When faced with suff ering, what are your choices? Answers to the problem of pain and tragedy often elude people of God. This sensitive book attempts to answer one of life's toughest questions. For those going through diffi cult circumstances, this book off ers a hopeful, scriptural approach that can help you through the storms of life. Endorsed by Joseph C. Aldrich, Ray Beeson, Dr. Daniel Juster. 176 pages.

| 9781880226865 | LB39 | $10.99 |

The Voice of the Lord *Messianic Jewish Daily Devotional*
—Edited by David J. Rudolph
Brings insight into the Jewish Scriptures—both Old and New Testaments. Twenty-two prominent Messianic contributors provide practical ways to apply biblical truth. Start your day with this unique resource. Explanatory notes. Perfect companion to the Complete Jewish Bible (see page 2). Endorsed by Edith Schaeff er, Dr. Arthur F. Glaser, Dr. Michael L. Brown, Mitch Glaser and Moishe Rosen. 416 pages.

| 9781880226704 | LB31 | $19.99 |

Kingdom Relationships *God's Laws for the Community of Faith*
—Dr. Ron Moseley
Focuses on the teaching of Torah—the Five Books of Moses—tapping into truths that greatly help modern-day members of the community of faith. 64 pages.

| 9781880226841 | LB37 | $8.99 |

His Names Are Wonderful
Getting to Know God Through His Hebrew Names
—Elizabeth L. Vander Meulen and Barbara D. Malda
In Hebrew thought, names did more than identify people; they revealed their nature. God's identity is expressed not in one name, but in many. This book will help readers know God better as they uncover the truths in his Hebrew names. 160 pages.

| 9781880226308 | LB58 | $9.99 |

Train Up A Child *Successful Parenting For The Next Generation*
—Dr. Daniel L. Switzer
The author, former principal of Ets Chaiyim Messianic Jewish Day School, and father of four, combines solid biblical teaching with Jewish sources on child raising, focusing on the biblical holy days, giving fresh insight into lling the role of parent. 188 pages. Endorsed by Dr. David J. Rudolph, Paul Lieberman, and Dr. David H. Stern.

| 9781880226377 | LB64 | $12.99 |

Fire on the Mountain - *Past Renewals, Present Revivals and the Coming Return of Israel*
—Dr. Louis Goldberg

The term "revival" is often used to describe a person or congregation turning to God. Is this something that "just happens," or can it be brought about? Dr. Louis Goldberg, author and former professor of Hebrew and Jewish Studies at Moody Bible Institute, examines real revivals that took place in Bible times and applies them to today. 268 pages.

9781880226858   **LB38** $15.99

Voices of Messianic Judaism *Confronting Critical Issues Facing a Maturing Movement*
—General Editor Rabbi Dan Cohn-Sherbok

Many of the best minds of the Messianic Jewish movement contributed their thoughts to this collection of 29 substantive articles. Challenging questions are debated: The involvement of Gentiles in Messianic Judaism? How should outreach be accomplished? Liturgy or not? Intermarriage? 256 pages.

781880226933   **LB46** $15.99

The Enduring Paradox *Exploratory Essays in Messianic Judaism*
—General Editor Dr. John Fischer

Yeshua and his Jewish followers began a new movement—Messianic Judaism—2,000 years ago. In the 20th century, it was reborn. Now, at the beginning of the 21st century, it is maturing. Twelve essays from top contributors to the theology of this vital movement of God, including: Dr. Walter C. Kaiser, Dr. David H. Stern, and Dr. John Fischer. 196 pages.

9781880226902   **LB43** $13.99

The World To Come *A Portal to Heaven on Earth*
—Derek Leman

An insightful book, exposing fallacies and false teachings surrounding this extremely important subject... paints a hopeful picture of the future and dispels many non-biblical notions. Intriguing chapters: Magic and Desire, The Vision of the Prophets, Hints of Heaven, Horrors of Hell, The Drama of the Coming Ages. Offers a fresh, but old, perspective on the world to come, as it interacts with the prophets of Israel and the Bible. 110 pages.

9781880226049   **LB67**   .$9.99

Hebrews Through a Hebrew's Eyes
—Dr. Stuart Sacks

Written to first-century Messianic Jews, this epistle, understood through Jewish eyes, edifies and encourages all. 119 pages. Endorsed by Dr. R.C. Sproul and James M. Boice.

9781880226612   **LB23** $10.99